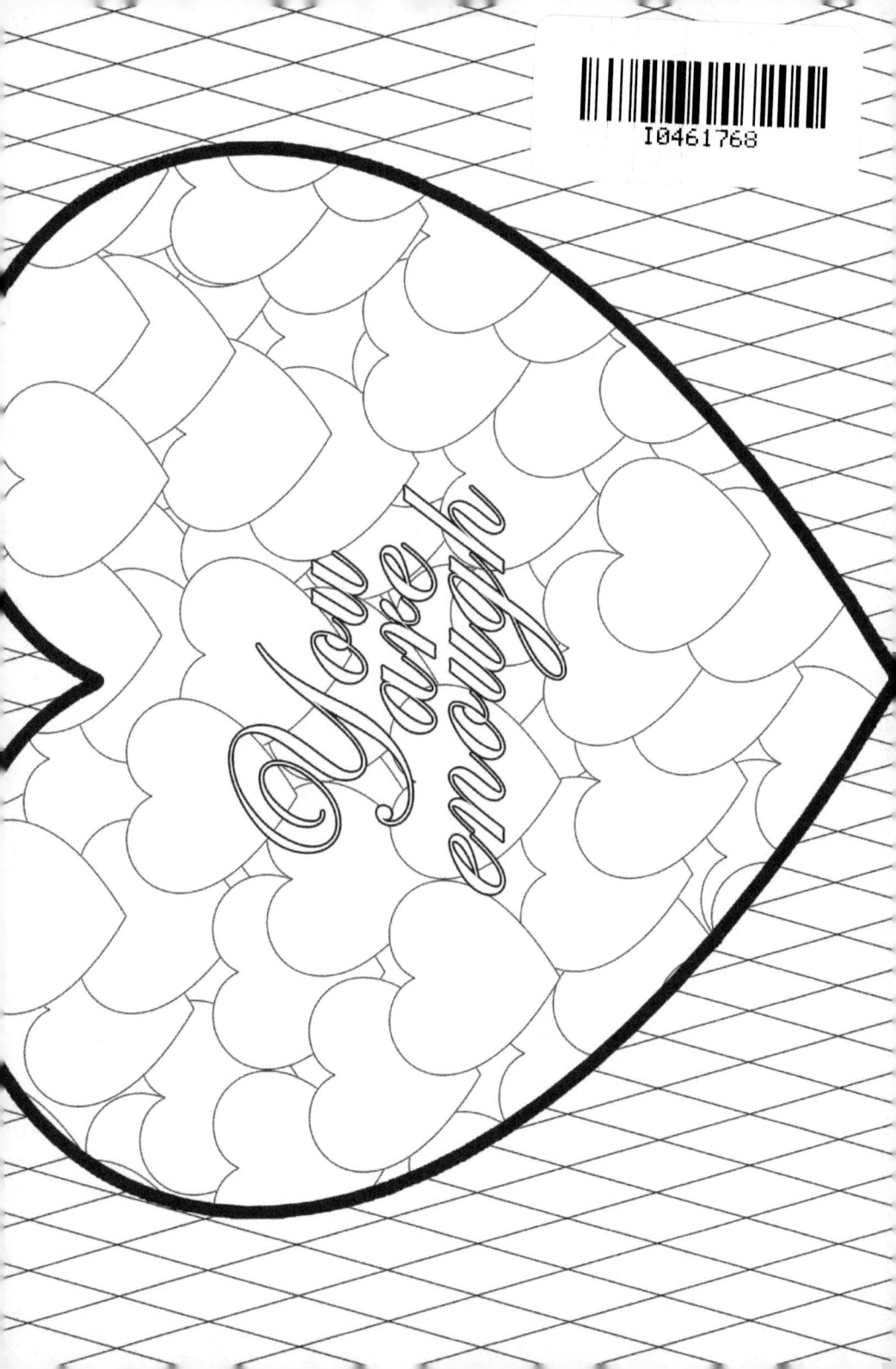

# Welcome to Mariko's first colouring book "Colouring Enoughness"

My journey with I-am-Enough started at the beginning of 2016. As suggested, I set my phone to tell me four times a day, for 100 days: "I am perfectly enough." The exercise promised to change my attitude for the better. It took about a week for the voice inside my head to associate the ring-tone with "I am perfectly enough."

Saying it in my head became easy. Saying, "You are enough," to a baby was easy. Continuing to believe it regardless of other people's opinions or external circumstances was another matter entirely! I also noticed how I was judging others as "not enough" for not meeting my expectations.

In addition to the phone alarm, I scattered notes around the house, including lipstick on the bathroom mirror. A week or two in, I started to experiment with photo editing on my phone, and it became a new hobby. I downloaded a number of photo editing and text apps, and occupied myself until the baby finally fell asleep.

With the confidence of 'being enough' came renewed energy and creativity, one result of which is this book.

Colouring books for adults suddenly became popular and they are available in numerous retail outlets, as well as from the artists themselves. Much has been written on the benefit of colouring; as a meditation practice, as a creative outlet, and of course as a self-care and me-time device.

My intention with leaving the letters that form 'I am enough' as an outline, is to give you the added benefit of repeating the words in your head. It has the potential to assist in improving your self-esteem, confidence, and self-worth, while you add colour to the pages.

I hope you enjoy "Colouring Enoughness."

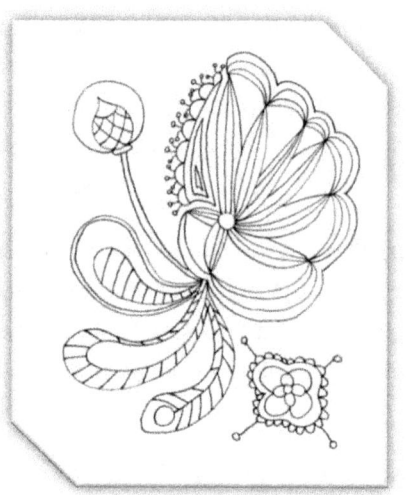

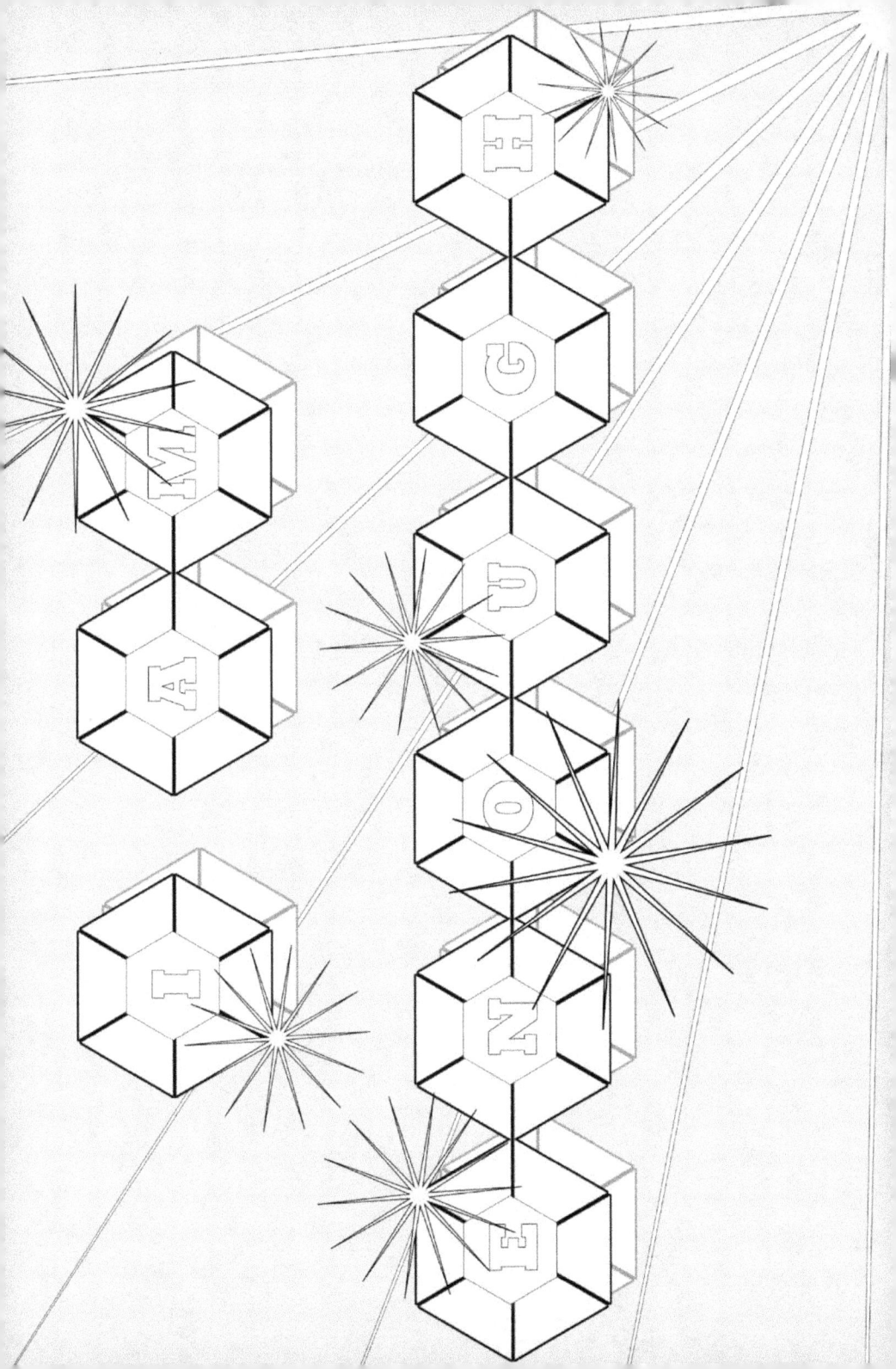

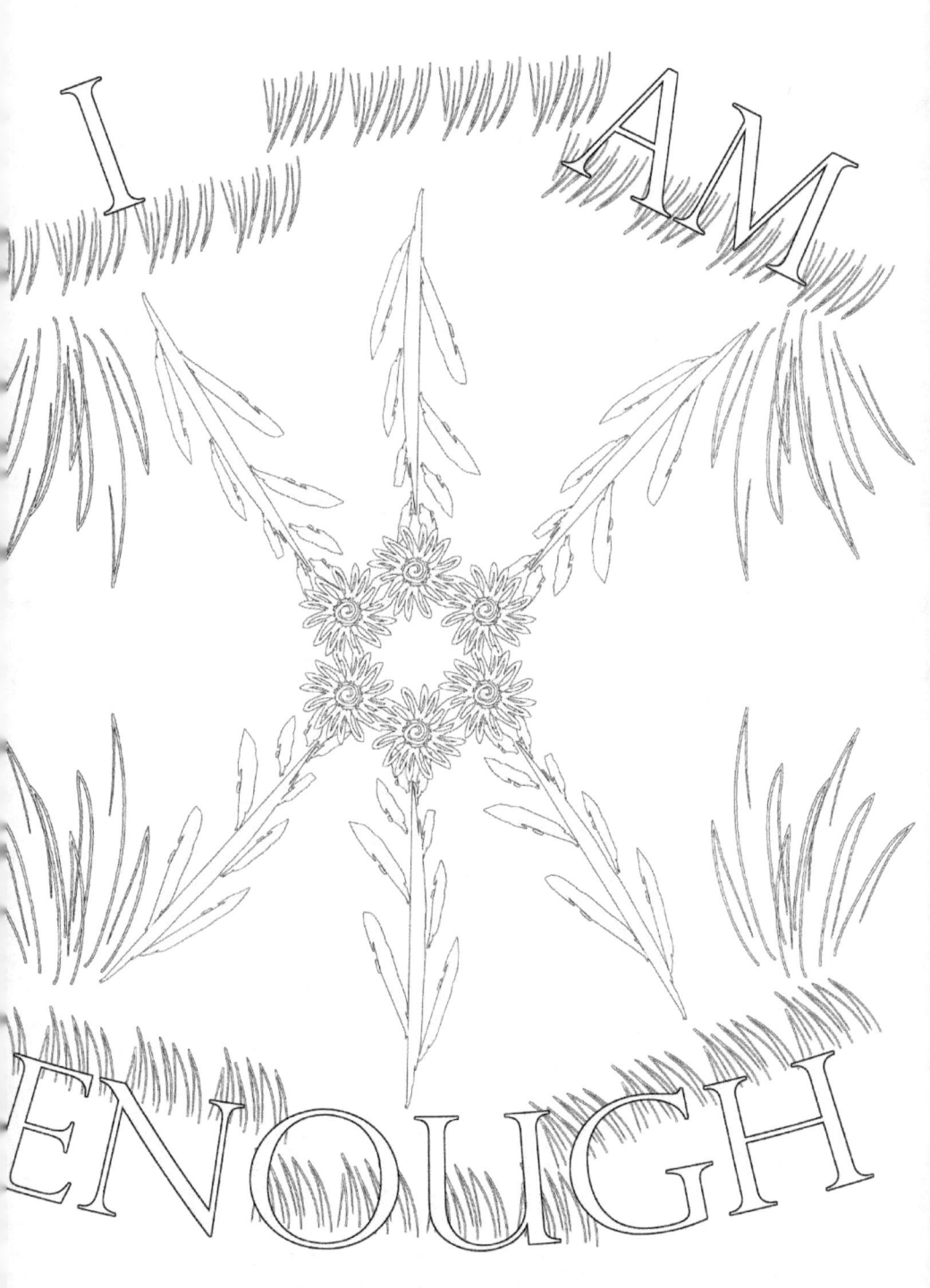

# I am enough

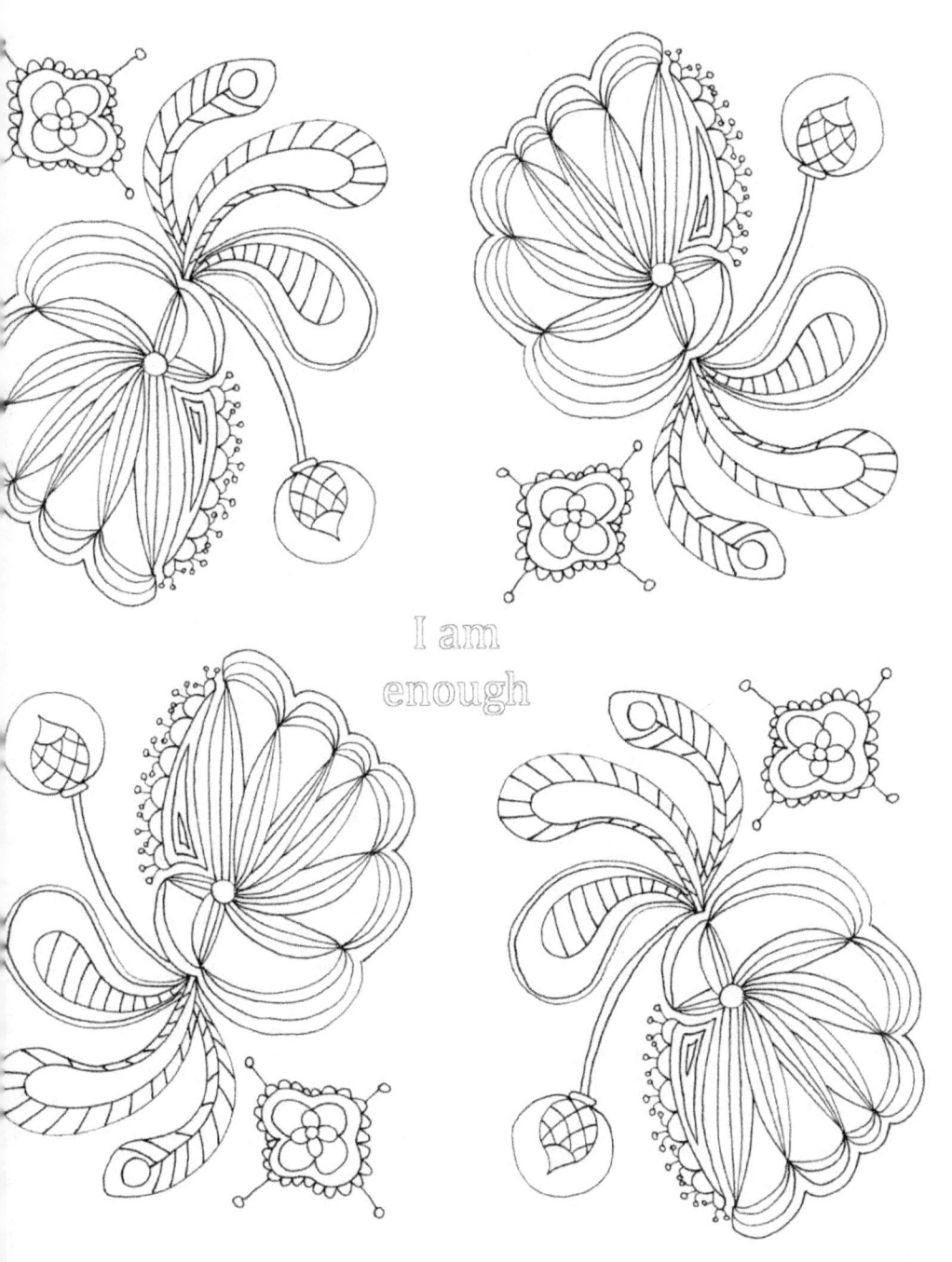

I am
enough

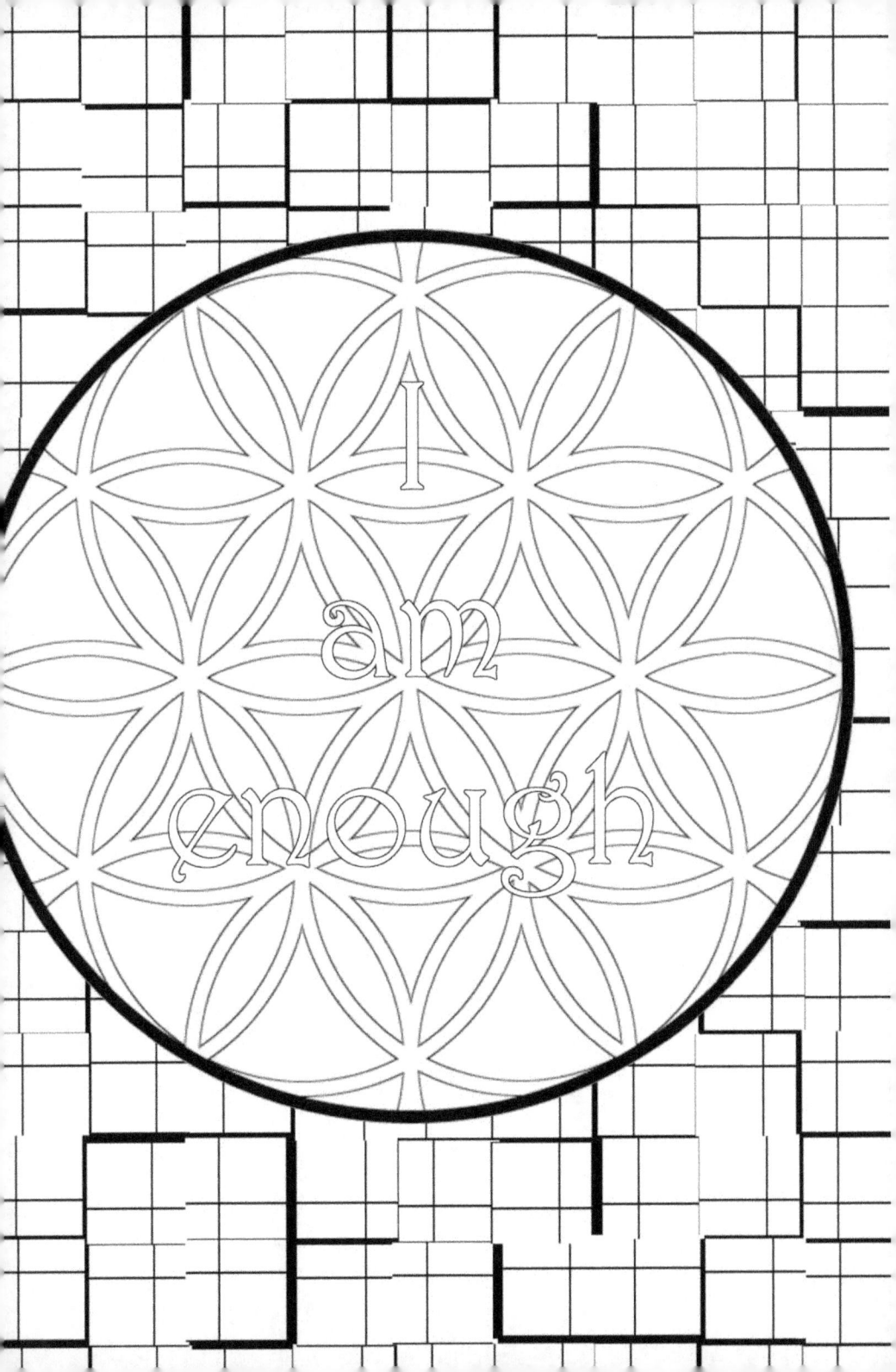

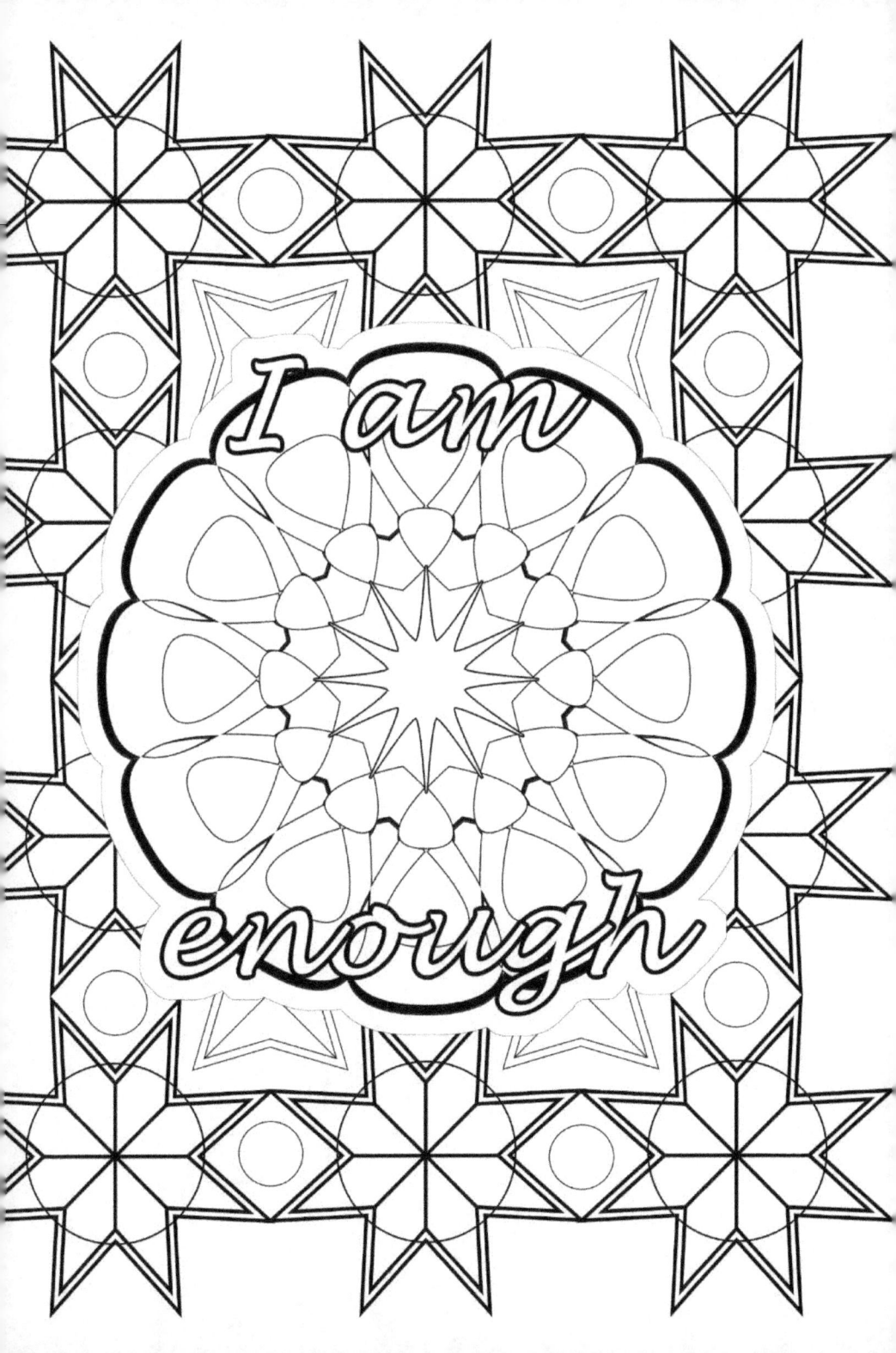

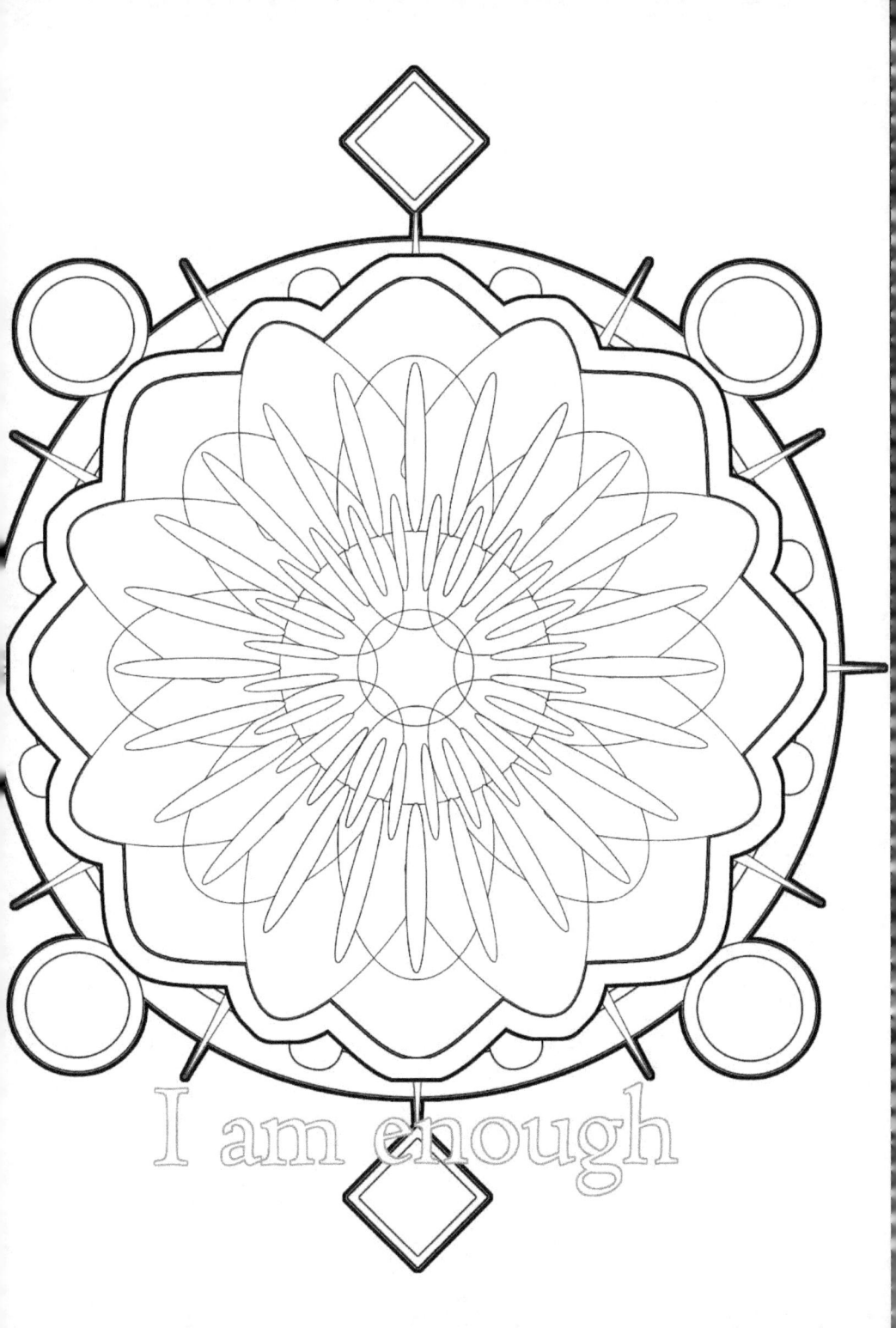

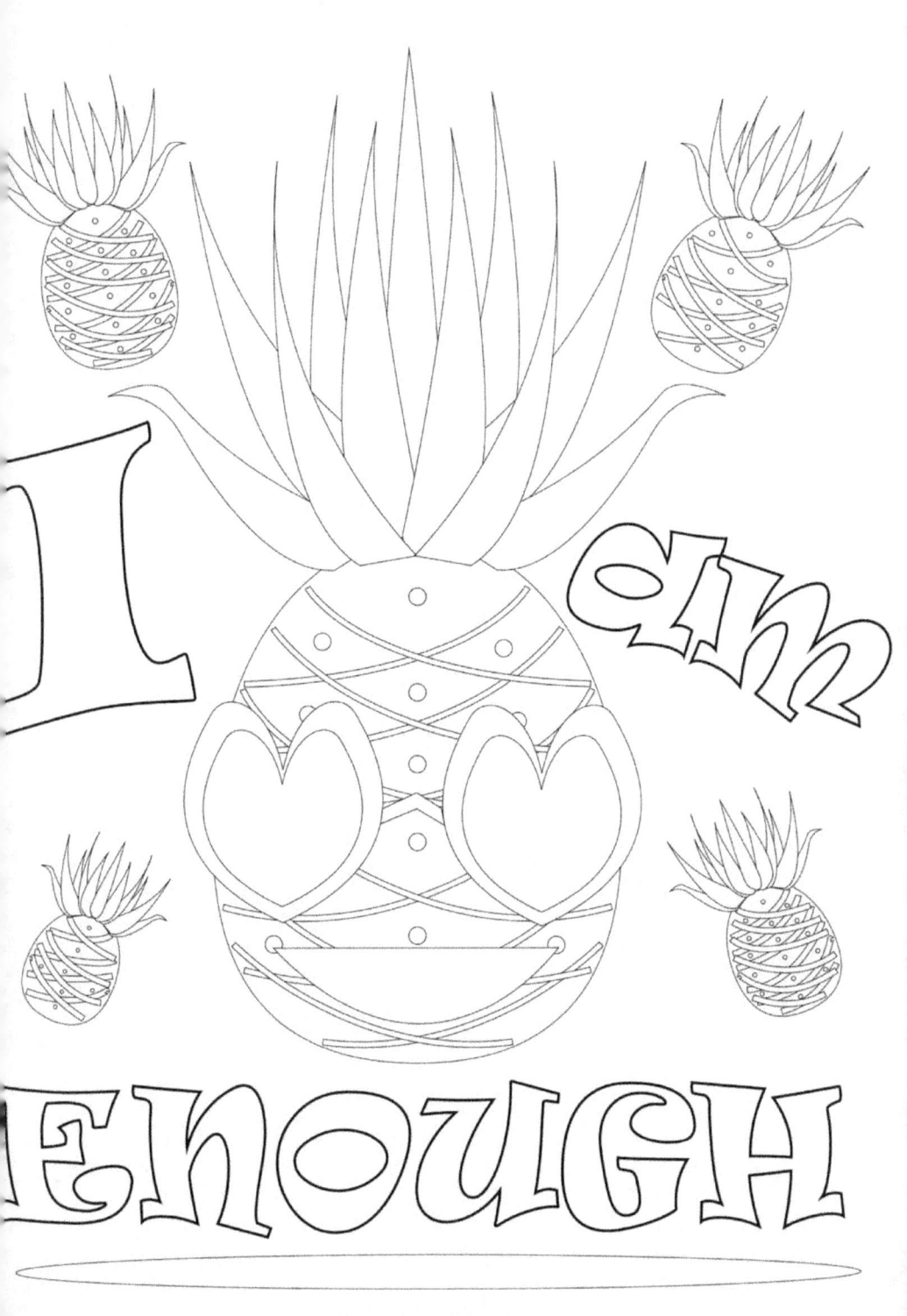

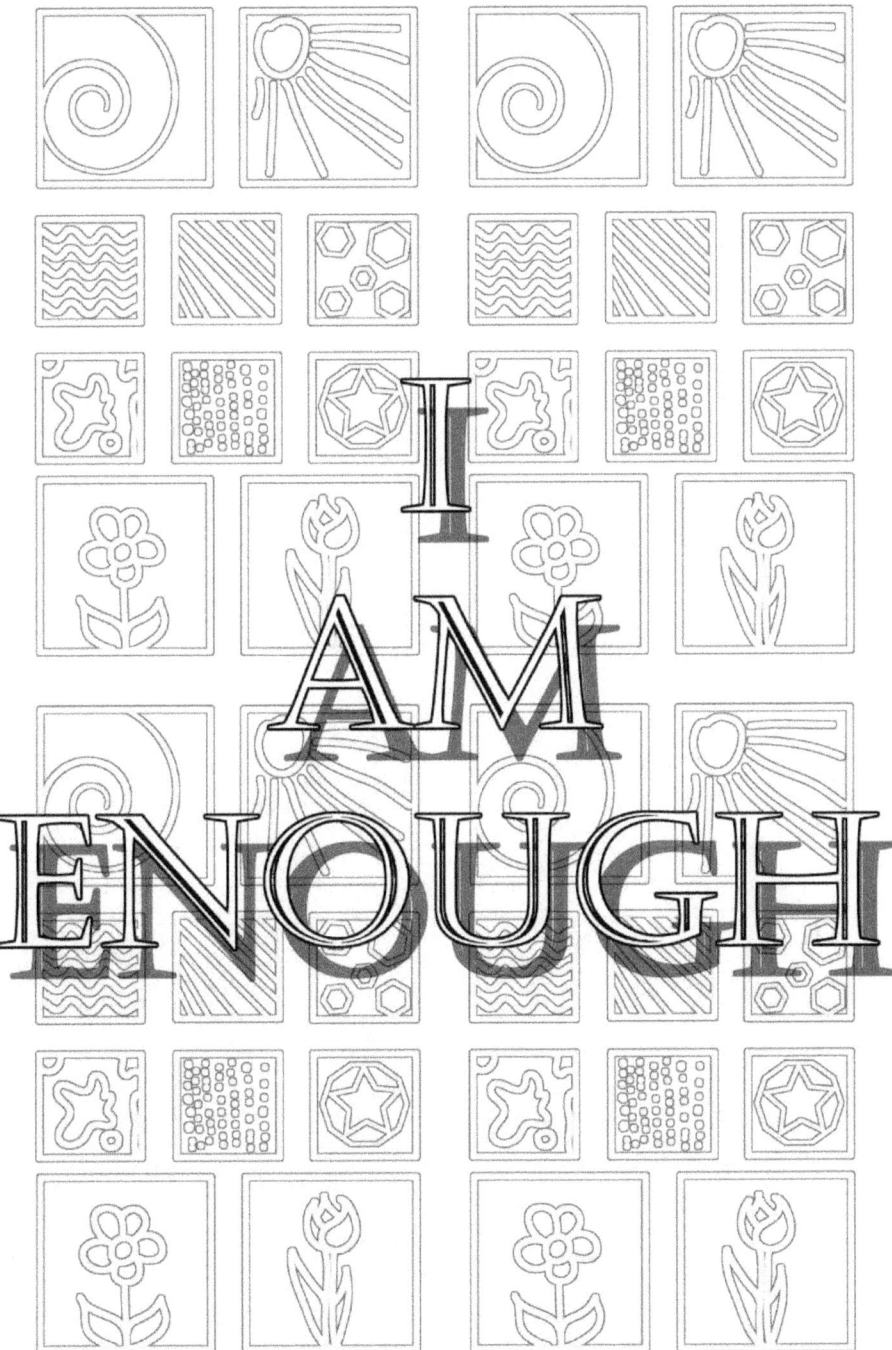

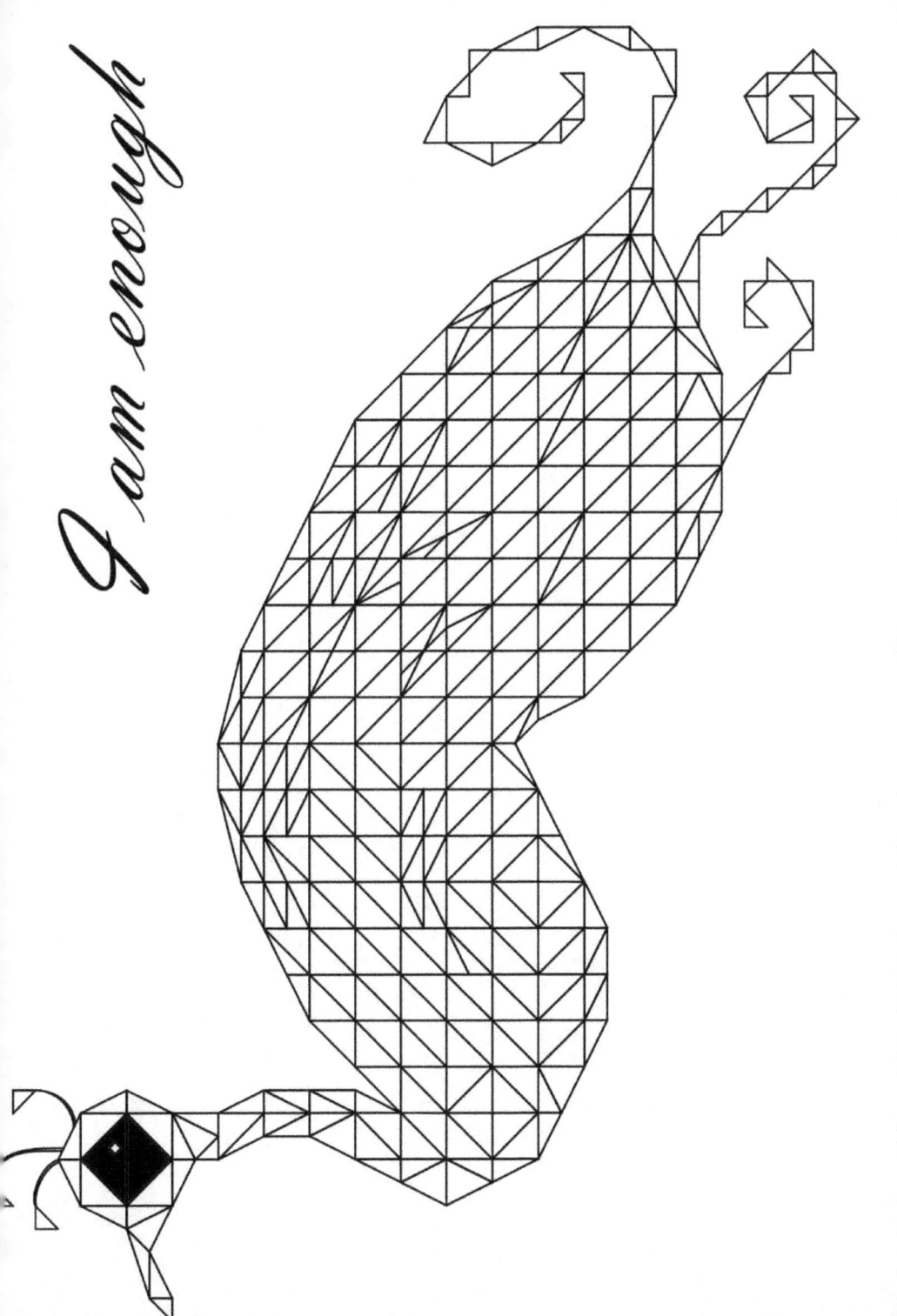

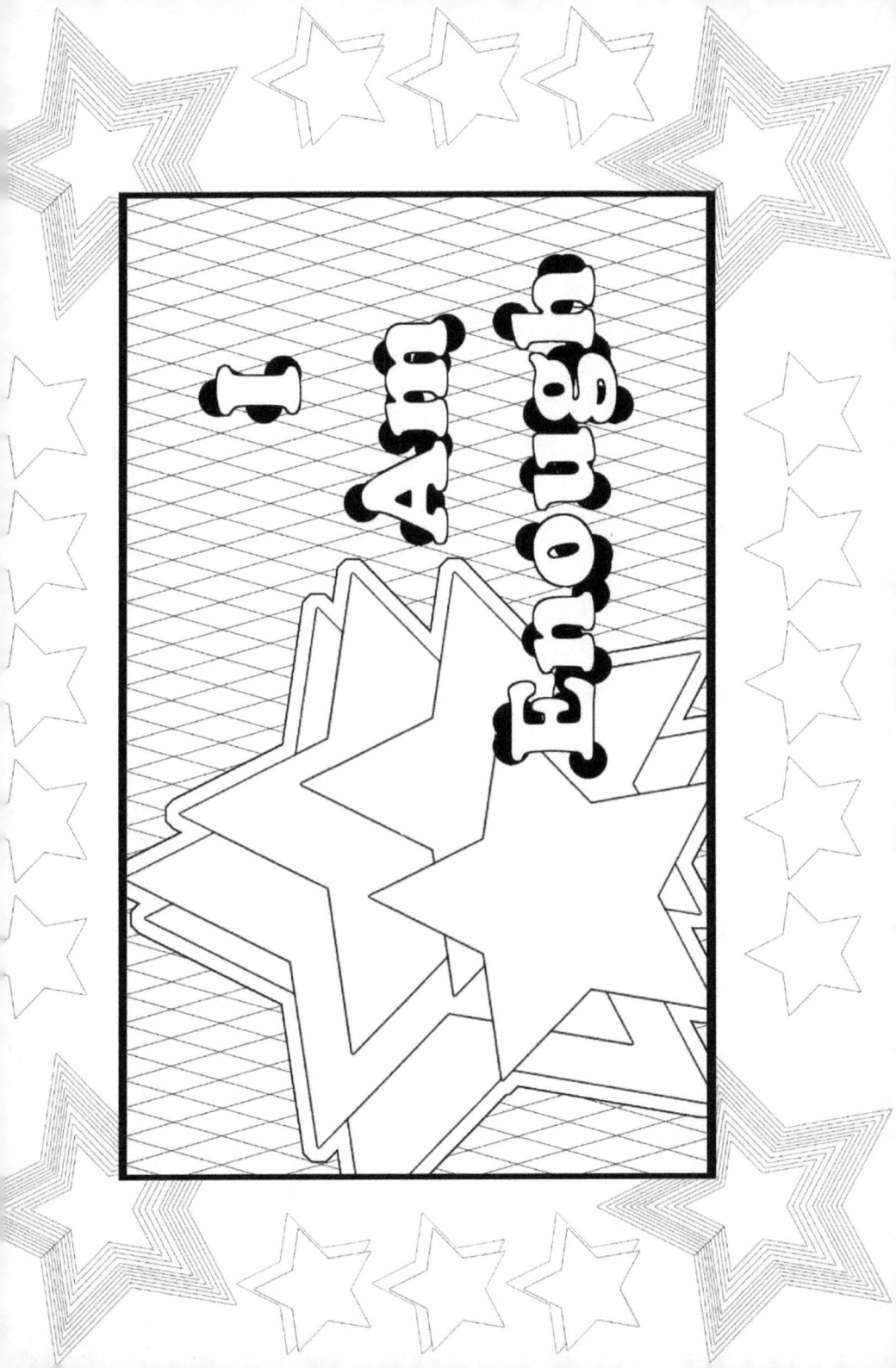

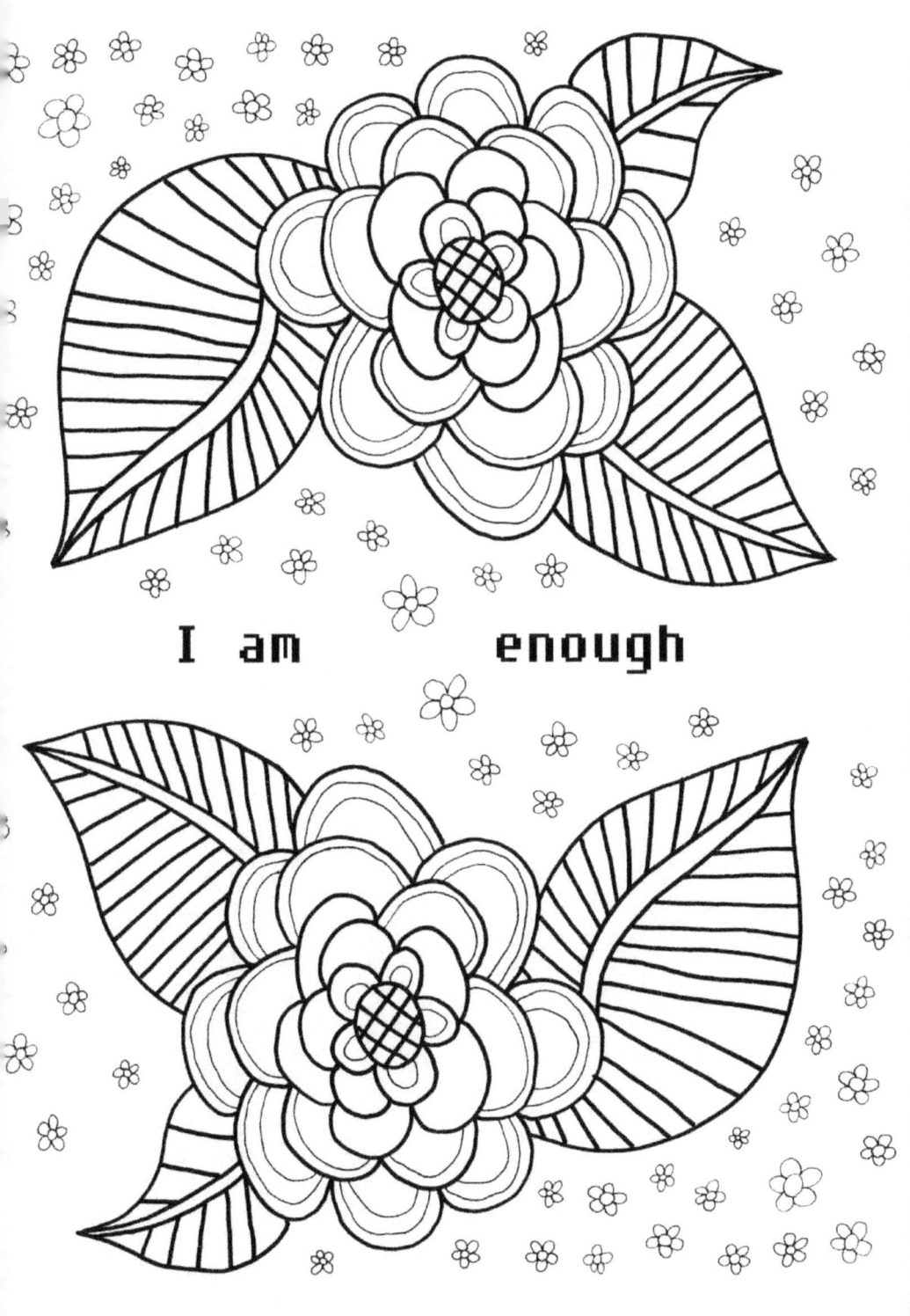

I am        enough

I am... enough

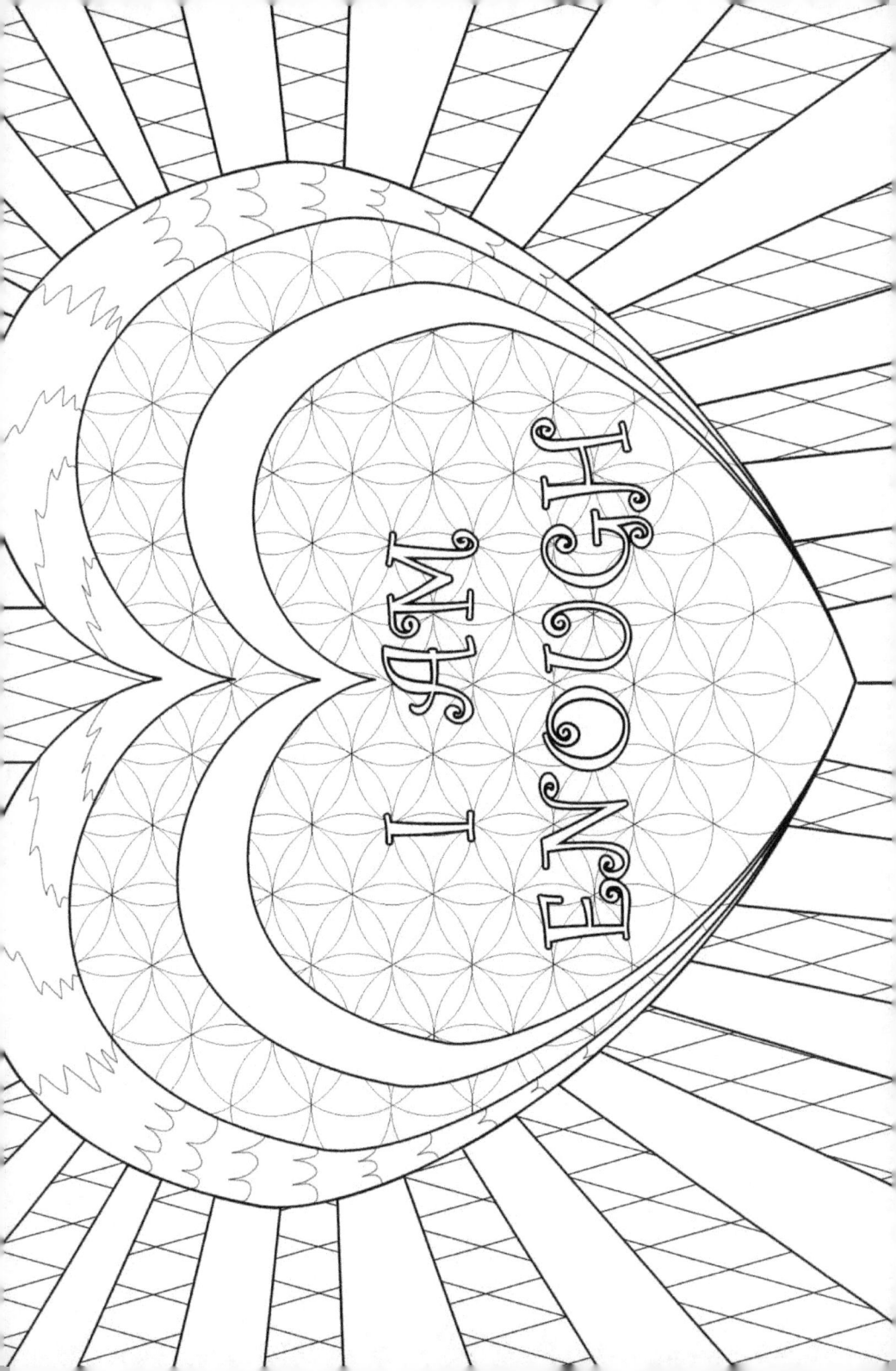

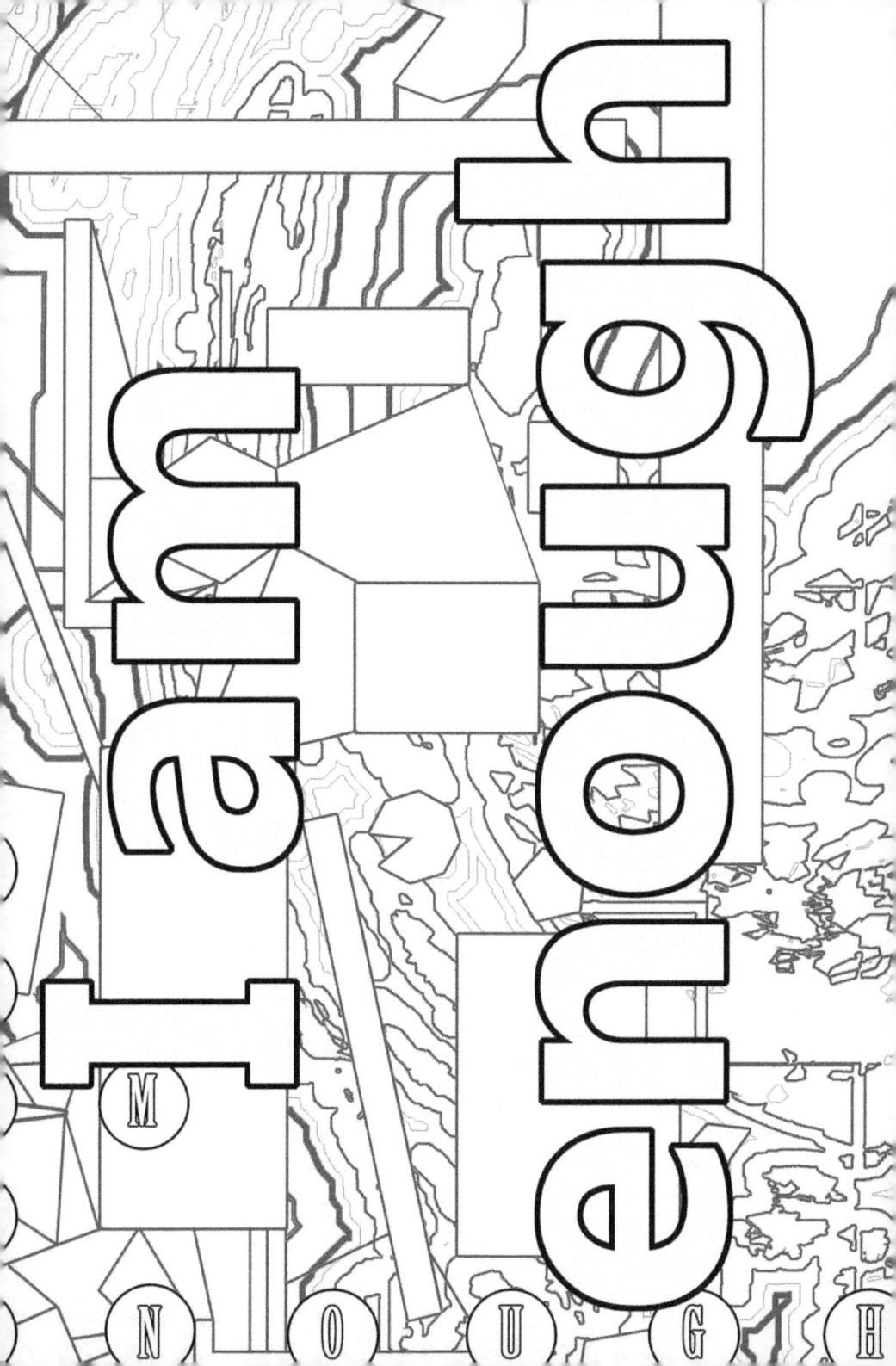

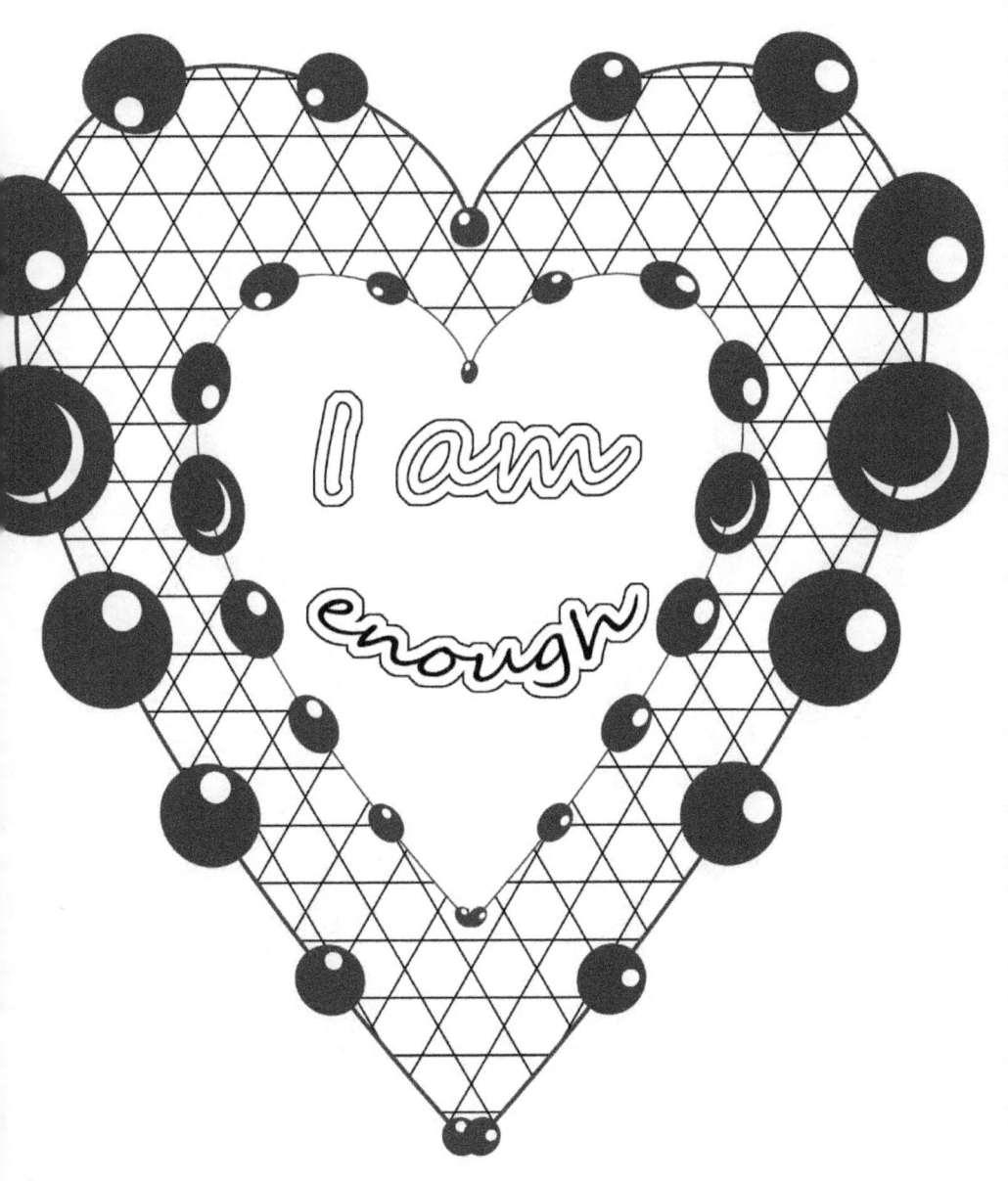

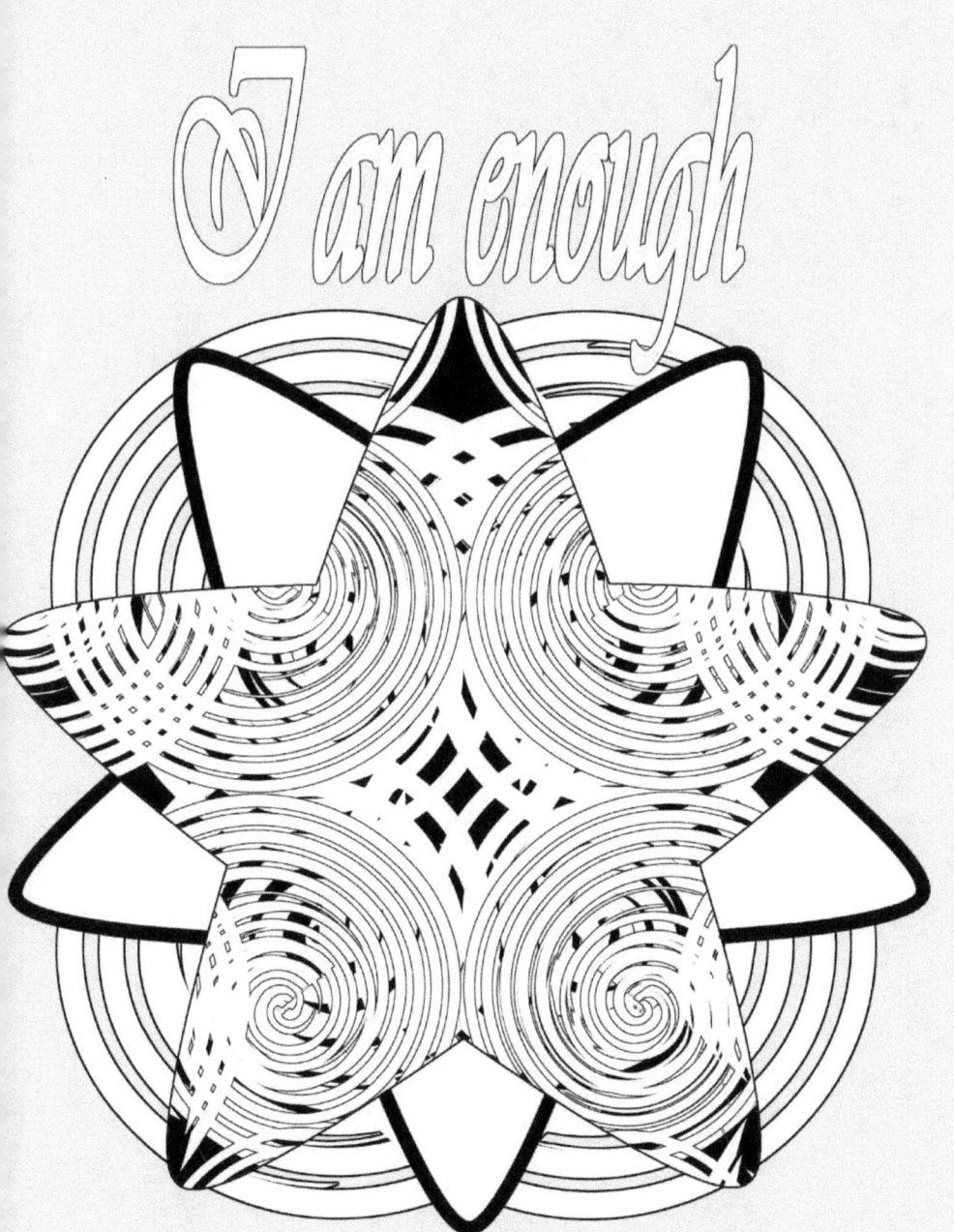

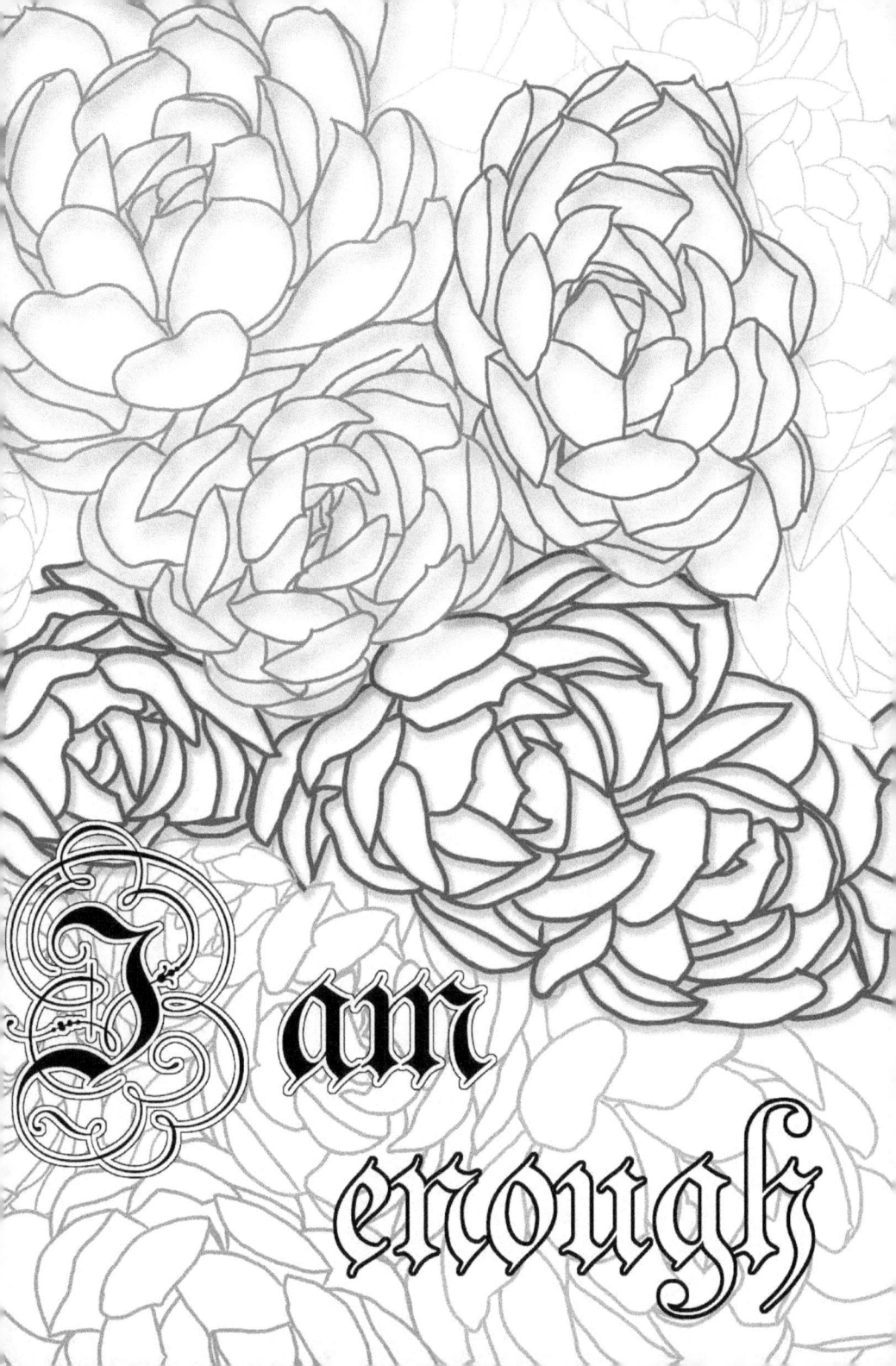

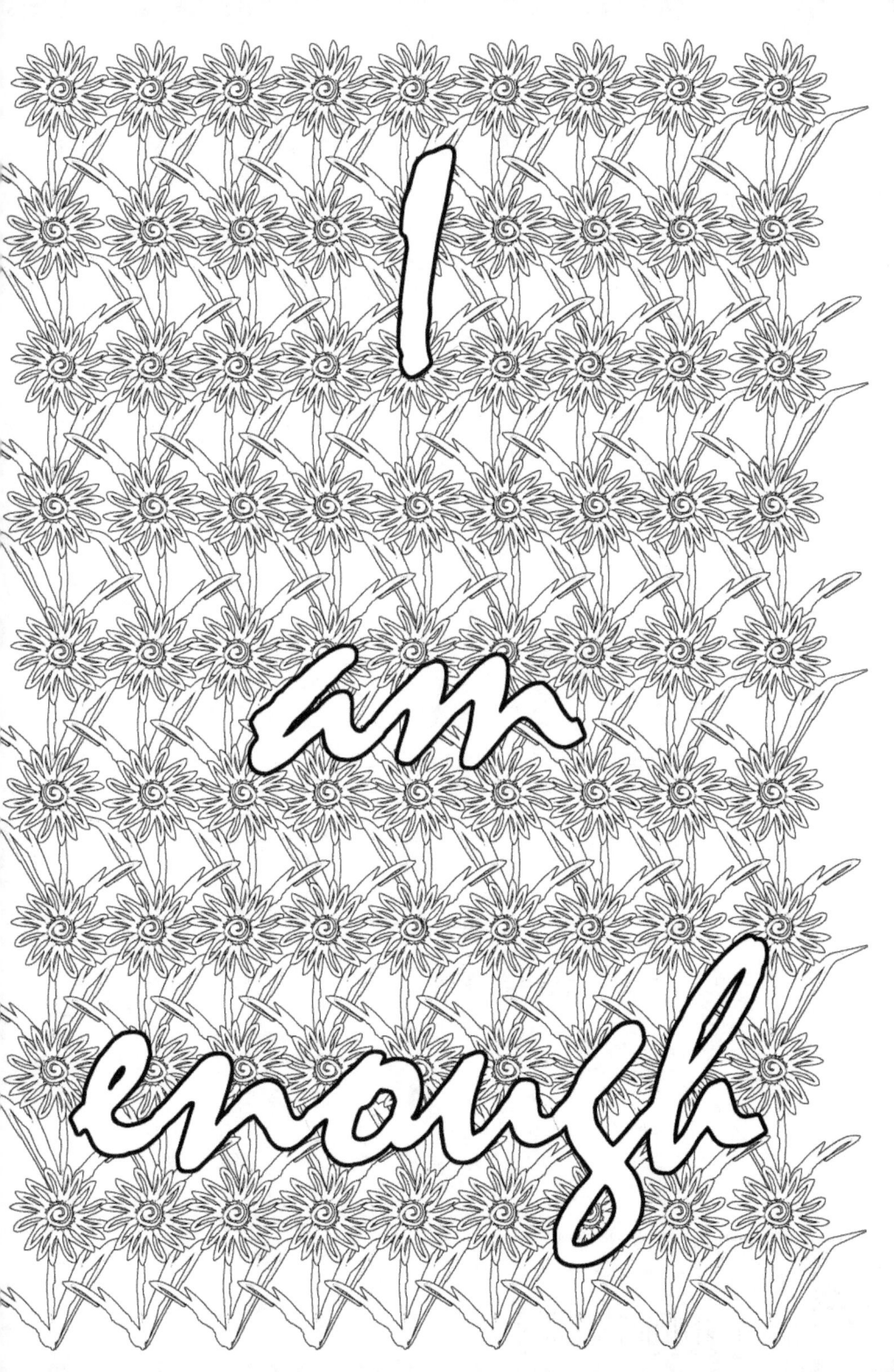

www.ingramcontent.com/pod-product-compliance
Lightning Source LLC
Chambersburg PA
CBHW061232180526
45170CB00003B/1259